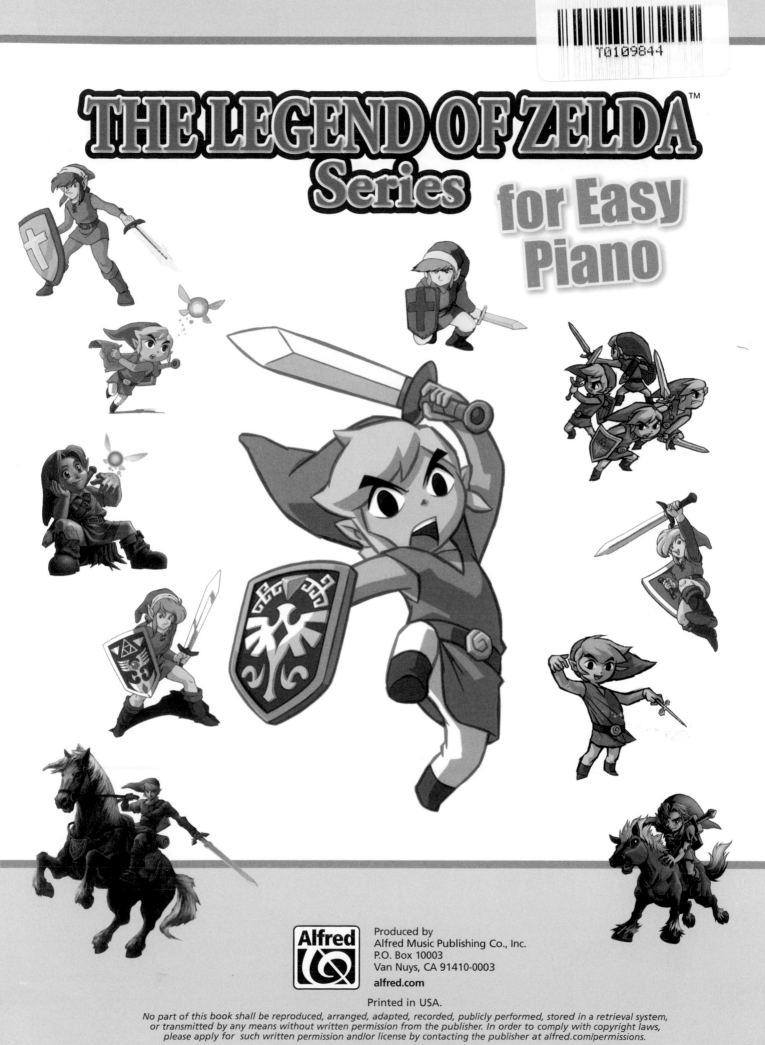

THE LEGEND OF ZELDA™ Series

for Easy Piano

Alfred

Produced by
Alfred Music Publishing Co., Inc.
P.O. Box 10003
Van Nuys, CA 91410-0003
alfred.com

Printed in USA.

ISBN-10: 0-7390-8324-4
ISBN-13: 978-0-7390-8324-6

TM and © 1986–2009 Nintendo

THE LEGEND OF ZELDA™
Series for Easy Piano

CONTENTS

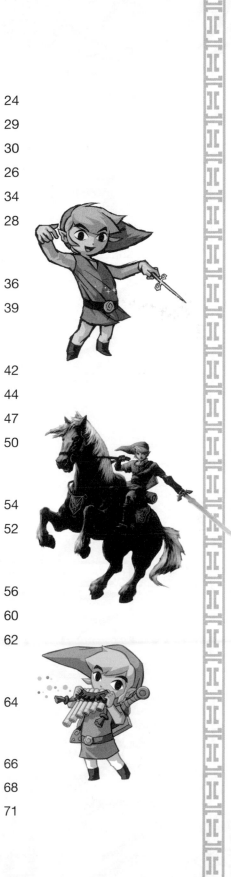

THE LEGEND OF ZELDA™:
TITLE THEME

Piano arrangement by SHINOBU AMAYAKE
Music supervision by NINTENDO

Composed by KOJI KONDO

(Original Key : B♭)
(Original Tempo : ♩ = 90)

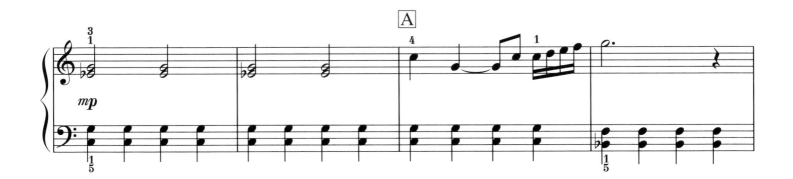

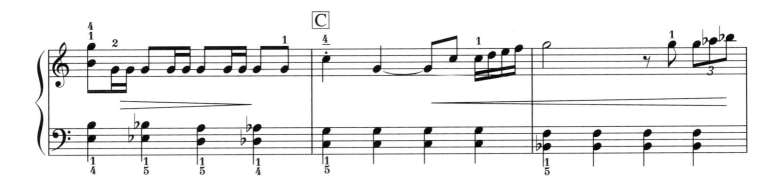

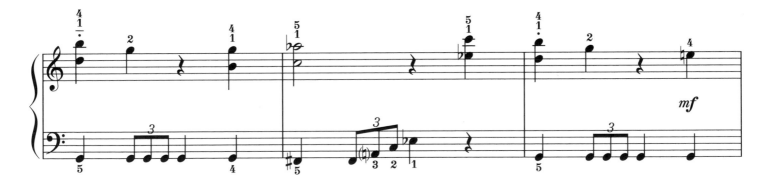

F.O.

THE LEGEND OF ZELDA™:
MAIN THEME

Piano arrangement by SHINOBU AMAYAKE
Music supervision by NINTENDO

Composed by KOJI KONDO

(Original Key : B♭)
(Original Tempo : ♩=150)

♩≒**100**

mf

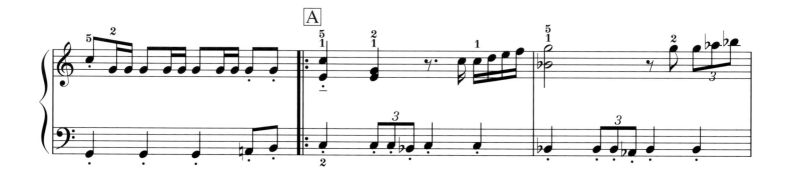

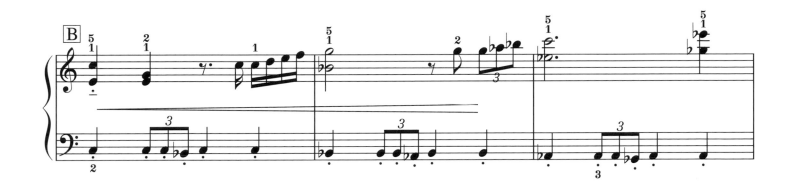

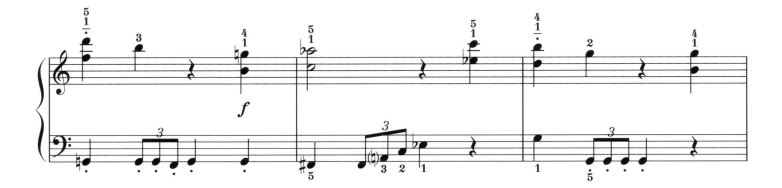

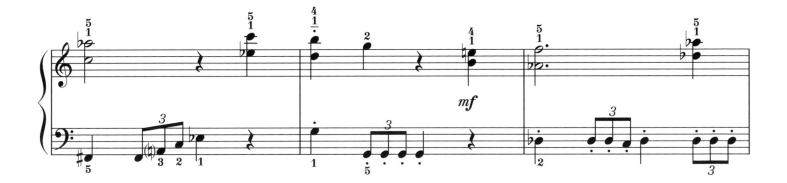

ZELDA II™: The Adventure of Link™
TITLE THEME

Piano arrangement by SHINOBU AMAYAKE
Music supervision by NINTENDO

Composed by AKITO NAKATSUKA

(Original Key : F)
(Original Tempo : ♩=112)

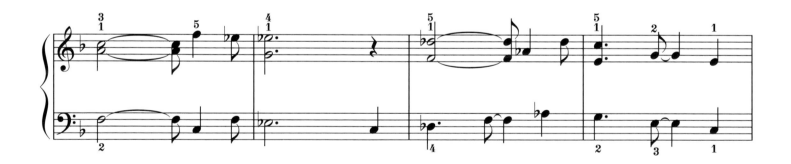

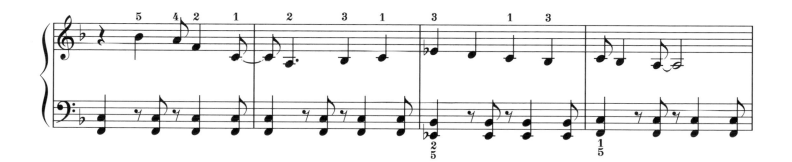

F.O.

ZELDA II™:
The Adventure of Link™
PALACE MUSIC

Piano arrangement by SHINOBU AMAYAKE
Music supervision by NINTENDO

Composed by AKITO NAKATSUKA

(Original Key : Gm)
(Original Tempo : ♩=150)

♩≒132

D.S.& F.O.

THE LEGEND OF ZELDA™:
A Link to the Past™
TITLE SCREEN

Piano arrangement by SHINOBU AMAYAKE
Music supervision by NINTENDO

Composed by KOJI KONDO

(Original Key : A♭)
(Original Tempo : ♩=104)

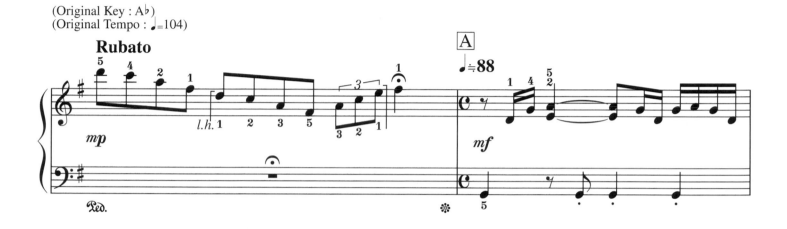

THE LEGEND OF ZELDA™:
A Link to the Past™
HYRULE CASTLE MUSIC

Piano arrangement by SHINOBU AMAYAKE
Music supervision by NINTENDO

Composed by KOJI KONDO

(Original Key : Gm)
(Original Tempo : ♩=135)

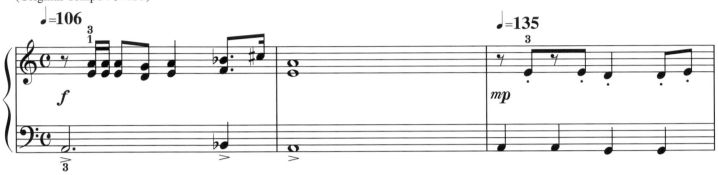

F.O.

THE LEGEND OF ZELDA™: *A Link to the Past*™
MAIN THEME

Piano arrangement by SHINOBU AMAYAKE
Music supervision by NINTENDO

Composed by KOJI KONDO

(Original Key : B♭)
(Original Tempo : ♩=137)

♩≒104

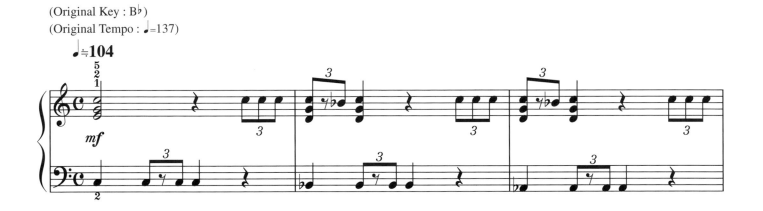

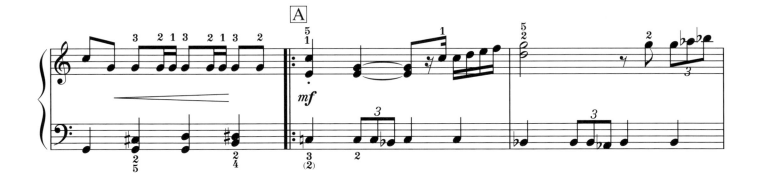

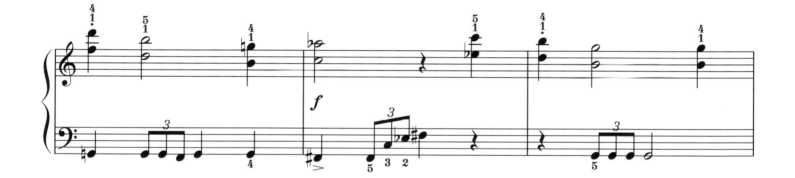

F.O.

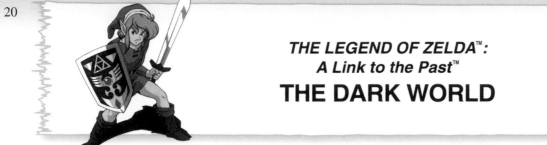

THE LEGEND OF ZELDA™:
A Link to the Past™
THE DARK WORLD

Piano arrangement by SHINOBU AMAYAKE
Music supervision by NINTENDO

Composed by KOJI KONDO

(Original Key : Cm)
(Original Tempo : ♩=137)

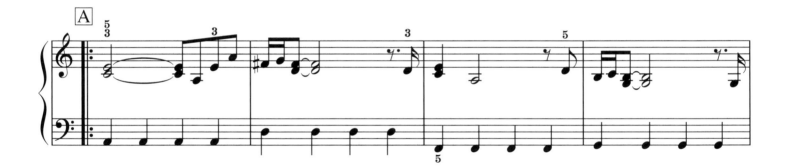

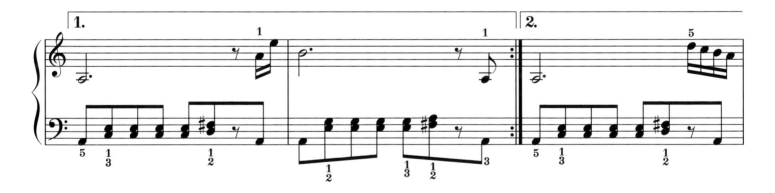

D.C.& F.O.

THE LEGEND OF ZELDA™:
Link's Awakening™
MAIN THEME

Piano arrangement by SHINOBU AMAYAKE
Music supervision by NINTENDO

Composed by KOJI KONDO and KOZUE ISHIKAWA

(Original Key : G)
(Original Tempo : ♩=150)

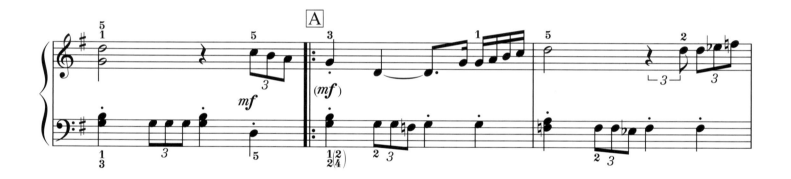

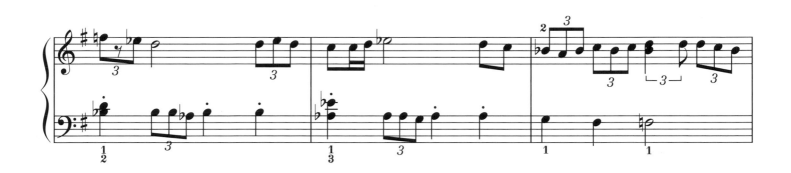

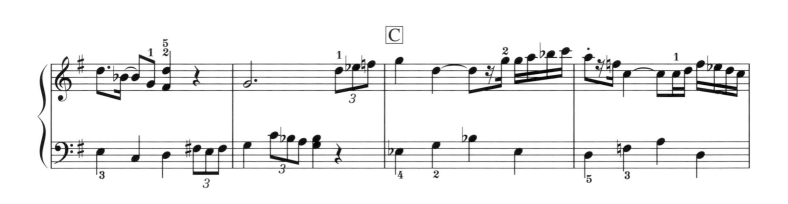

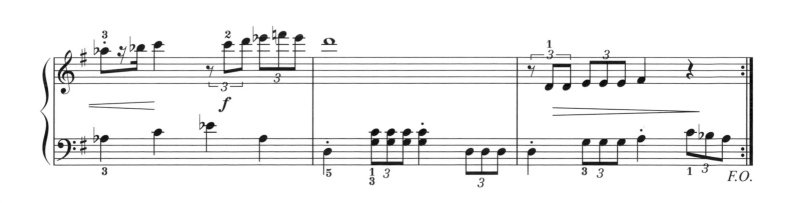

F.O.

THE LEGEND OF ZELDA™:
Ocarina of Time™
TITLE THEME

Piano arrangement by SHINOBU AMAYAKE
Music supervision by NINTENDO

Composed by KOJI KONDO

(Original Key : C)
(Original Tempo : ♩=74)

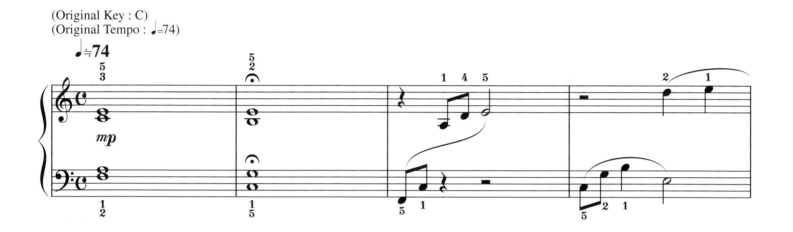

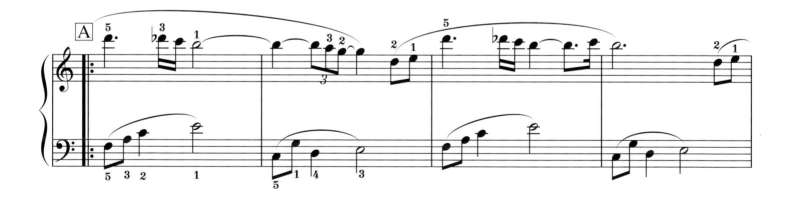

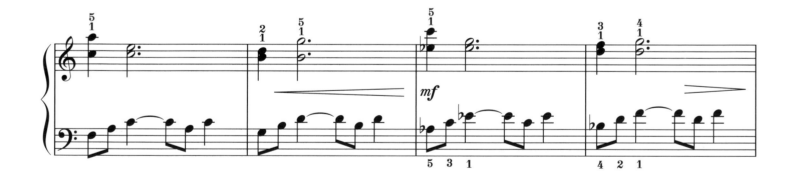

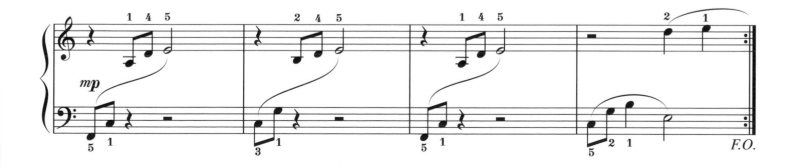

F.O.

THE LEGEND OF ZELDA™:
Ocarina of Time™
LOST WOODS (SARIA'S SONG)

Piano arrangement by SHINOBU AMAYAKE
Music supervision by NINTENDO

Composed by KOJI KONDO

(Original Key : C)
(Original Tempo : ♩=140)

♩≒**120**

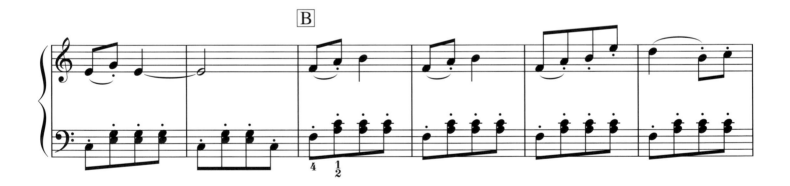

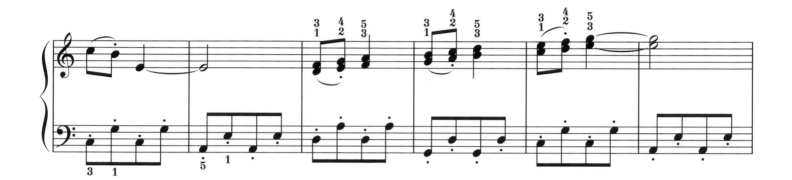

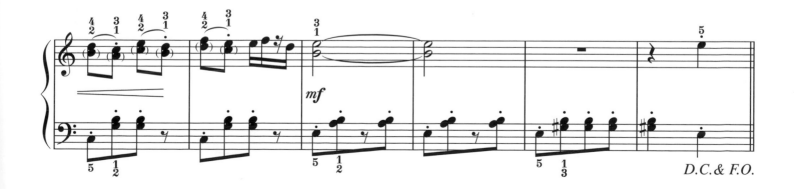

D.C.& F.O.

THE LEGEND OF ZELDA™:
Ocarina of Time™
SONG OF STORMS

Piano arrangement by SHINOBU AMAYAKE
Music supervision by NINTENDO

Composed by KOJI KONDO

(Original Key : Dm)
(Original Tempo : ♩=200)

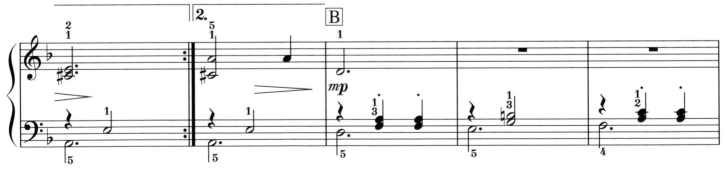

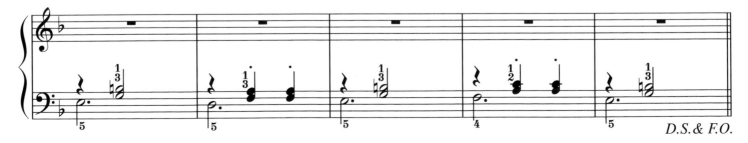

D.S.& F.O.

THE LEGEND OF ZELDA™:
Ocarina of Time™
PRINCESS ZELDA'S THEME

Composed by KOJI KONDO
Piano arrangement by SHINOBU AMAYAKE
Music supervision by NINTENDO

(Original Key : G)
(Original Tempo : ♩=110)

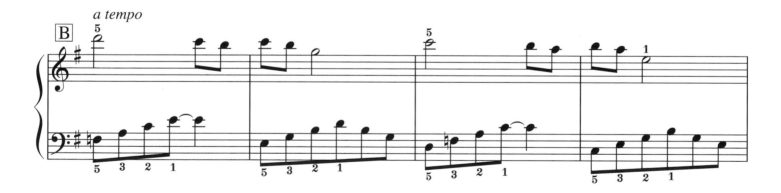

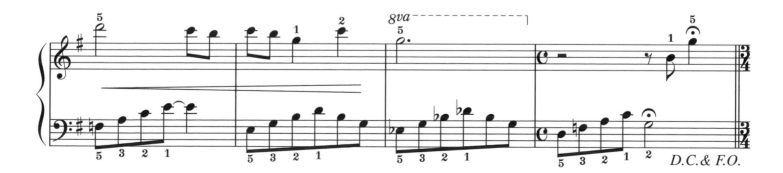

D.C.& F.O.

THE LEGEND OF ZELDA™:
Ocarina of Time™
HYRULE FIELD

Piano arrangement by SHINOBU AMAYAKE
Music supervision by NINTENDO

Composed by KOJI KONDO

(Original Key : G)
(Original Tempo : ♩=150)

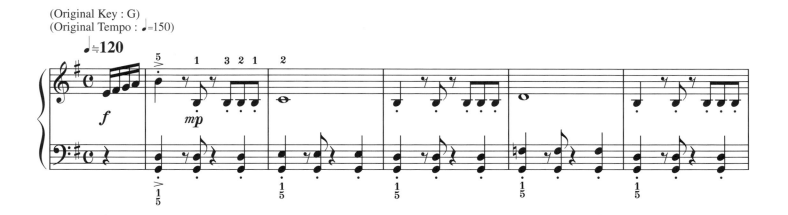

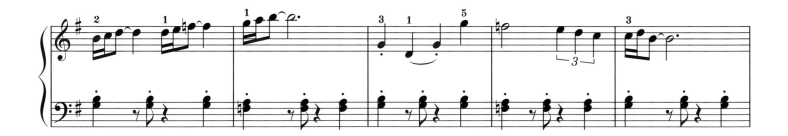

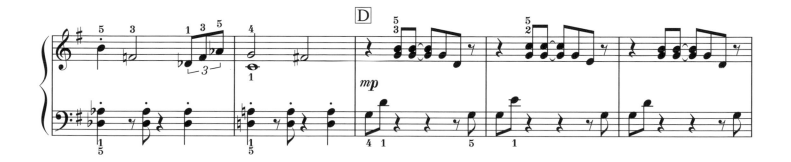

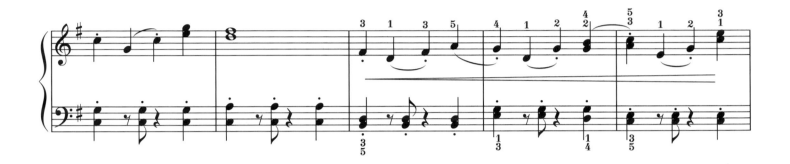

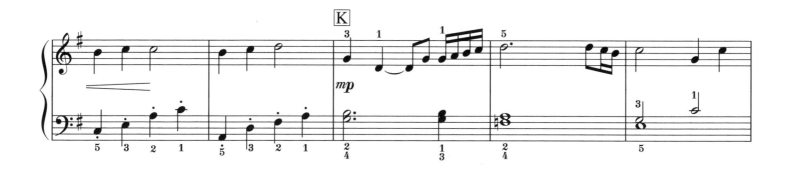

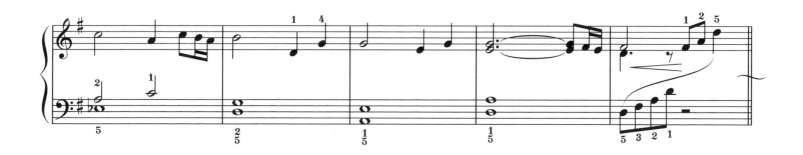

THE LEGEND OF ZELDA™:
Ocarina of Time™
GERUDO VALLEY

Piano arrangement by SHINOBU AMAYAKE
Music supervision by NINTENDO

Composed by KOJI KONDO

(Original Key : F♯m)
(Original Tempo : ♩=120)

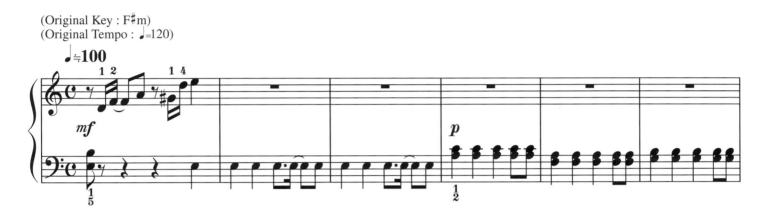

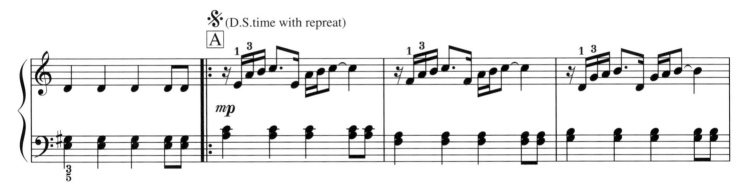

D.S.& F.O.

THE LEGEND OF ZELDA™:
Majora's Mask™
PRELUDE OF MAJORA'S MASK

Piano arrangement by SHINOBU AMAYAKE
Music supervision by NINTENDO

Composed by KOJI KONDO

(Original Key : D)
(Original Tempo : ♩.=94)

♩.≒ **84**

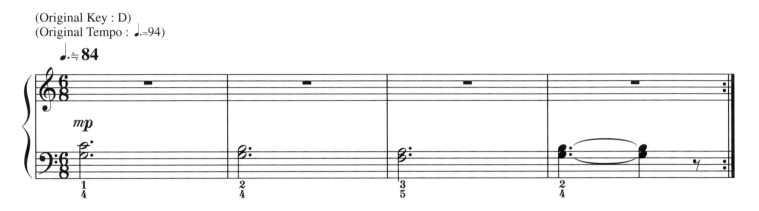

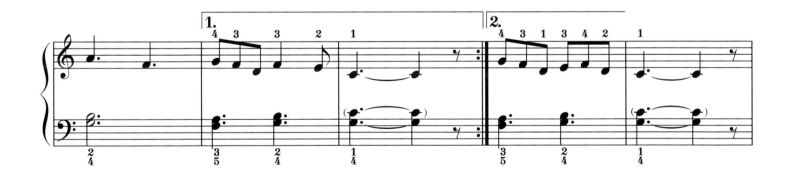

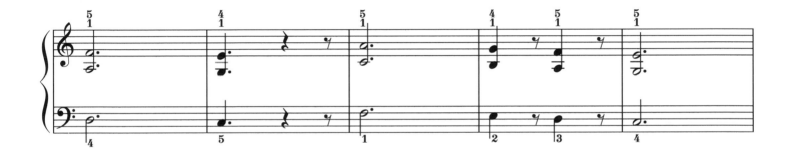

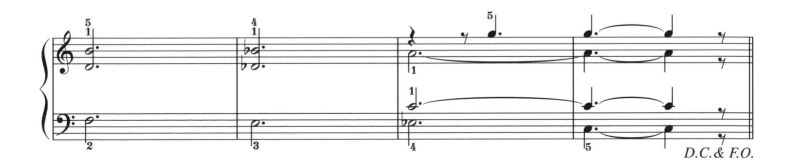

D.C.& F.O.

THE LEGEND OF ZELDA™:
Majora's Mask™
TERMINA FIELD

Piano arrangement by SHINOBU AMAYAKE
Music supervision by NINTENDO

Composed by KOJI KONDO

(Original Key : Gm)
(Original Tempo : ♩=100)

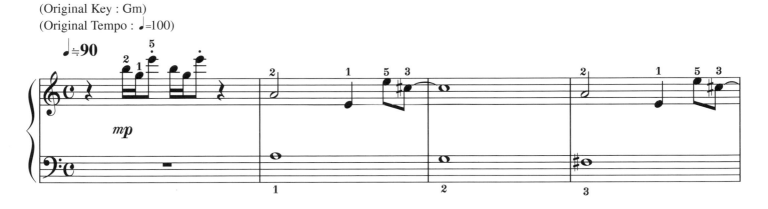

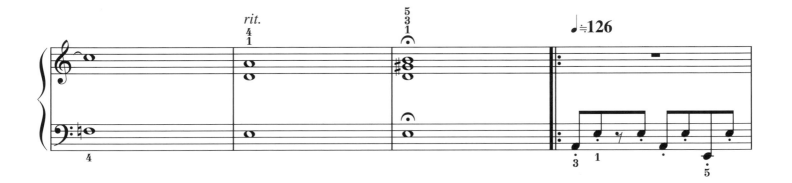

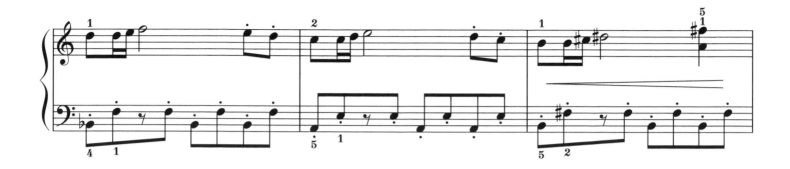

B

C

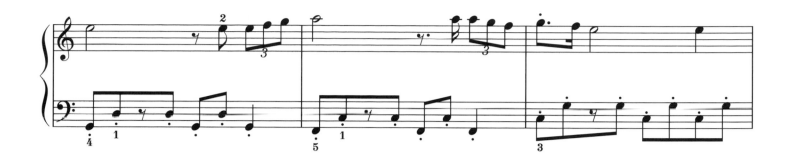

F.O.

THE LEGEND OF ZELDA™:
The Wind Waker™
MAIN THEME

Piano arrangement by SHINOBU AMAYAKE
Music supervision by NINTENDO

Composed by KENTA NAGATA

(Original Key : D♭)
(Original Tempo : ♩.=120)

♩.≒108

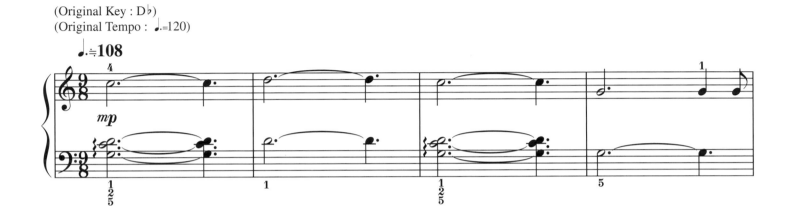

D.S. & F.O.

THE LEGEND OF ZELDA™:
The Wind Waker™
DRAGON ROOST ISLAND

Piano arrangement by SHINOBU AMAYAKE
Music supervision by NINTENDO

Composed by KENTA NAGATA

(Original Key : Gm)
(Original Tempo : ♩=172)

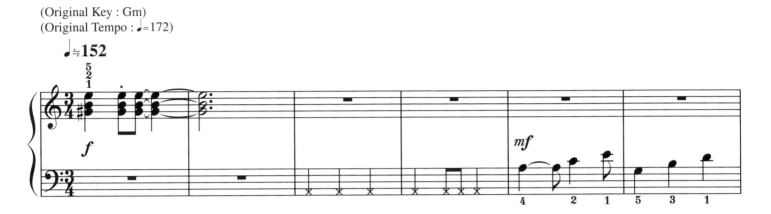

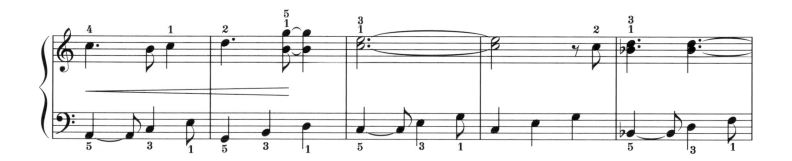

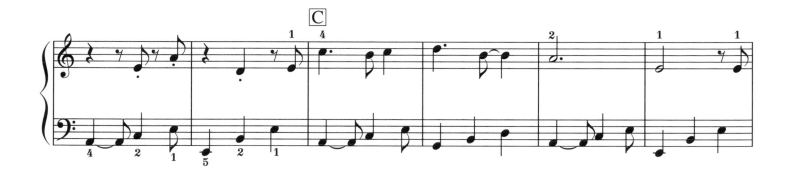

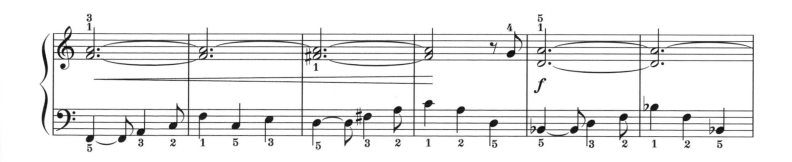

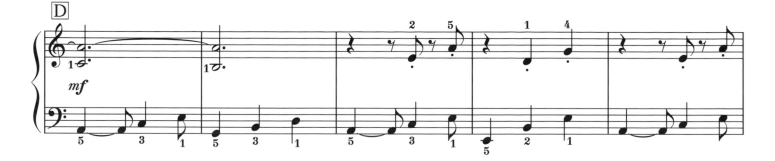

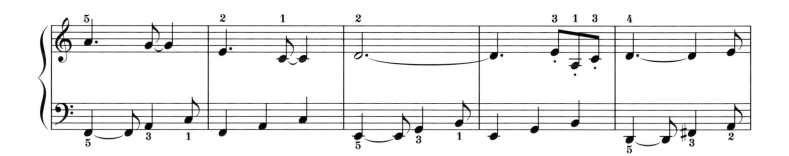

F.O.

THE LEGEND OF ZELDA™:
The Wind Waker™
OCEAN THEME

Piano arrangement by SHINOBU AMAYAKE
Music supervision by NINTENDO

Composed by KENTA NAGATA

(Original Key : D)
(Original Tempo : ♩=140)

♩≒120

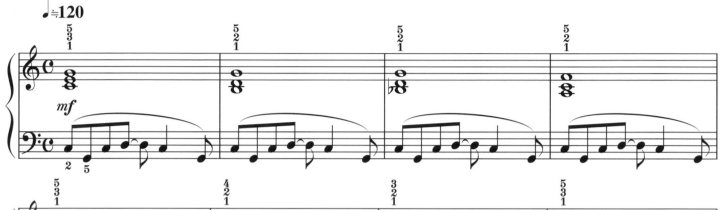

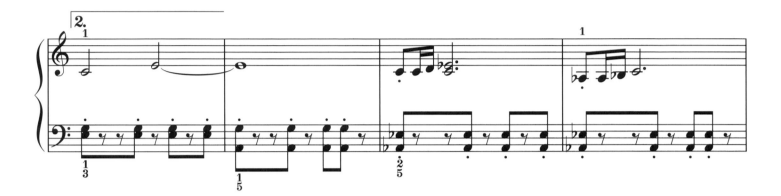

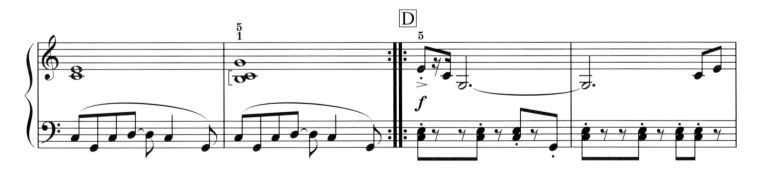

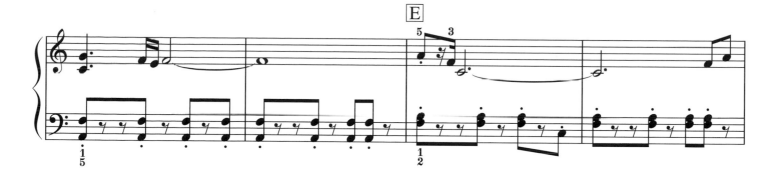

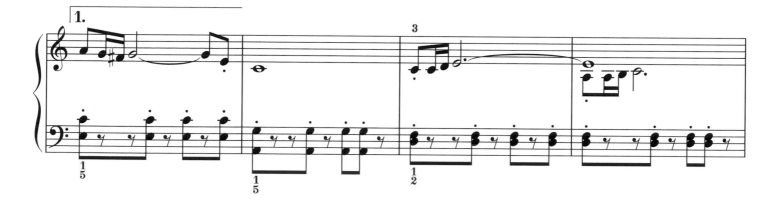

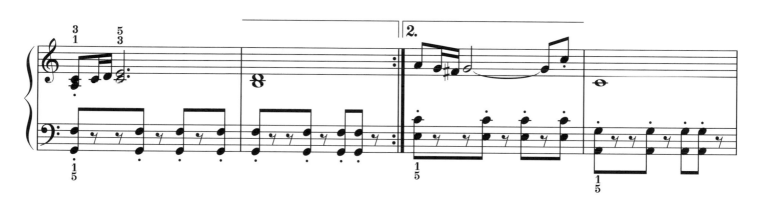

D.S.& F.O.

THE LEGEND OF ZELDA™:
The Wind Waker™
MOLGERA

Piano arrangement by SHINOBU AMAYAKE
Music supervision by NINTENDO

Composed by HAJIME WAKAI

(Original Key : Em)
(Original Tempo : ♩=149)

♩≒120

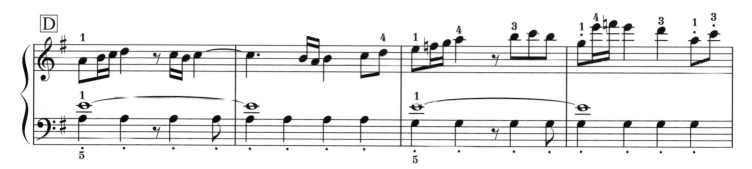

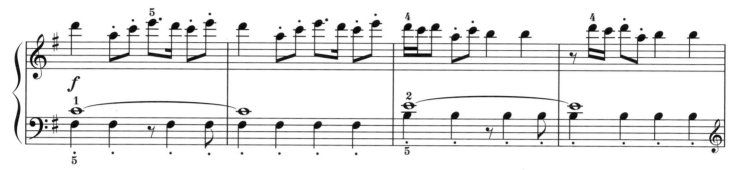

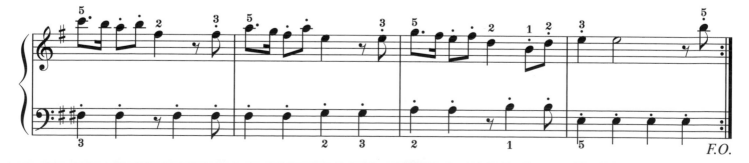

F.O.

THE LEGEND OF ZELDA™:
Four Swords Adventures
FIELD THEME

Piano arrangement by SHINOBU AMAYAKE
Music supervision by NINTENDO

Composed by ASUKA OHTA

(Original Key : G)
(Original Tempo : ♩=144)

♩≒**120**

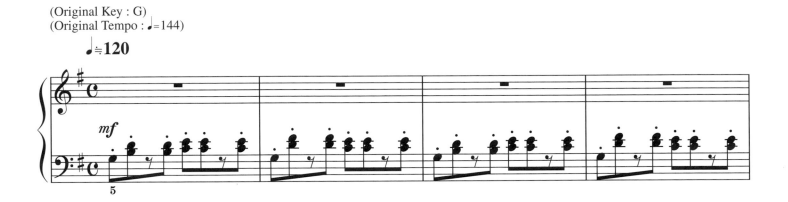

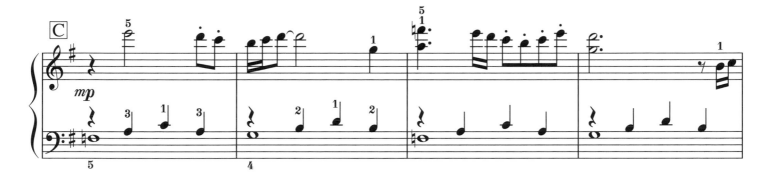

C

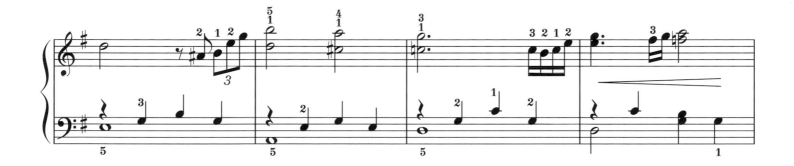

D

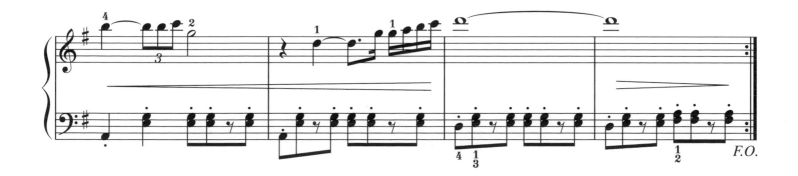

F.O.

THE LEGEND OF ZELDA™:
Four Swords Adventures
VILLAGE OF THE BLUE
MAIDEN RESTORED

Piano arrangement by SHINOBU AMAYAKE
Music supervision by NINTENDO

Composed by KOJI KONDO and ASUKA OHTA

(Original Key : B♭)
(Original Tempo : ♩=140)

♩≒120

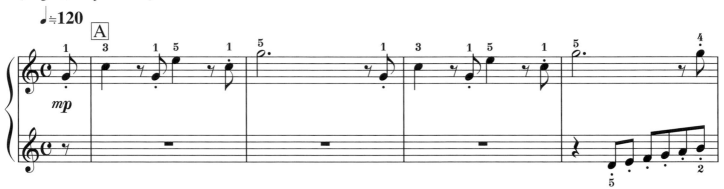

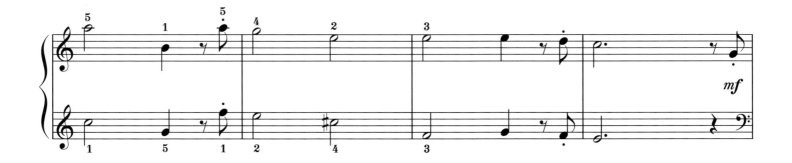

D.S.& F.O.

THE LEGEND OF ZELDA™:
Twilight Princess
HYRULE FIELD MAIN THEME

Piano arrangement by SHINOBU AMAYAKE
Music supervision by NINTENDO

Composed by TORU MINEGISHI

(Original Key : Em)
(Original Tempo : ♩=144)

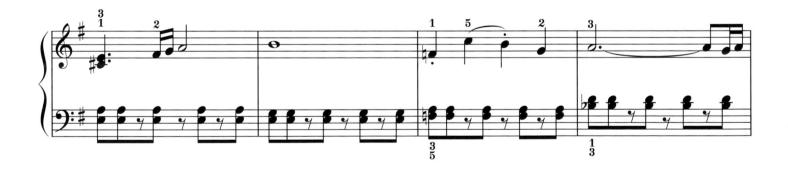

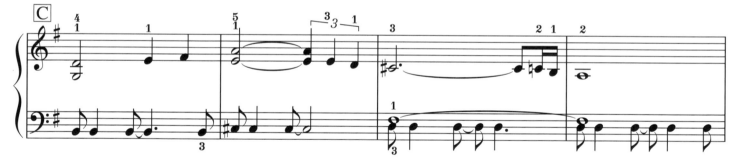

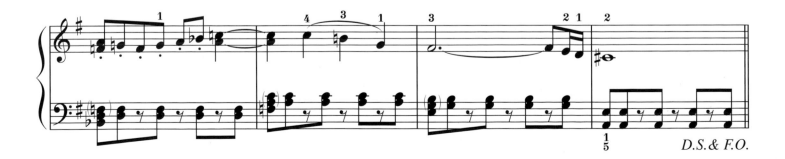

D.S.& F.O.

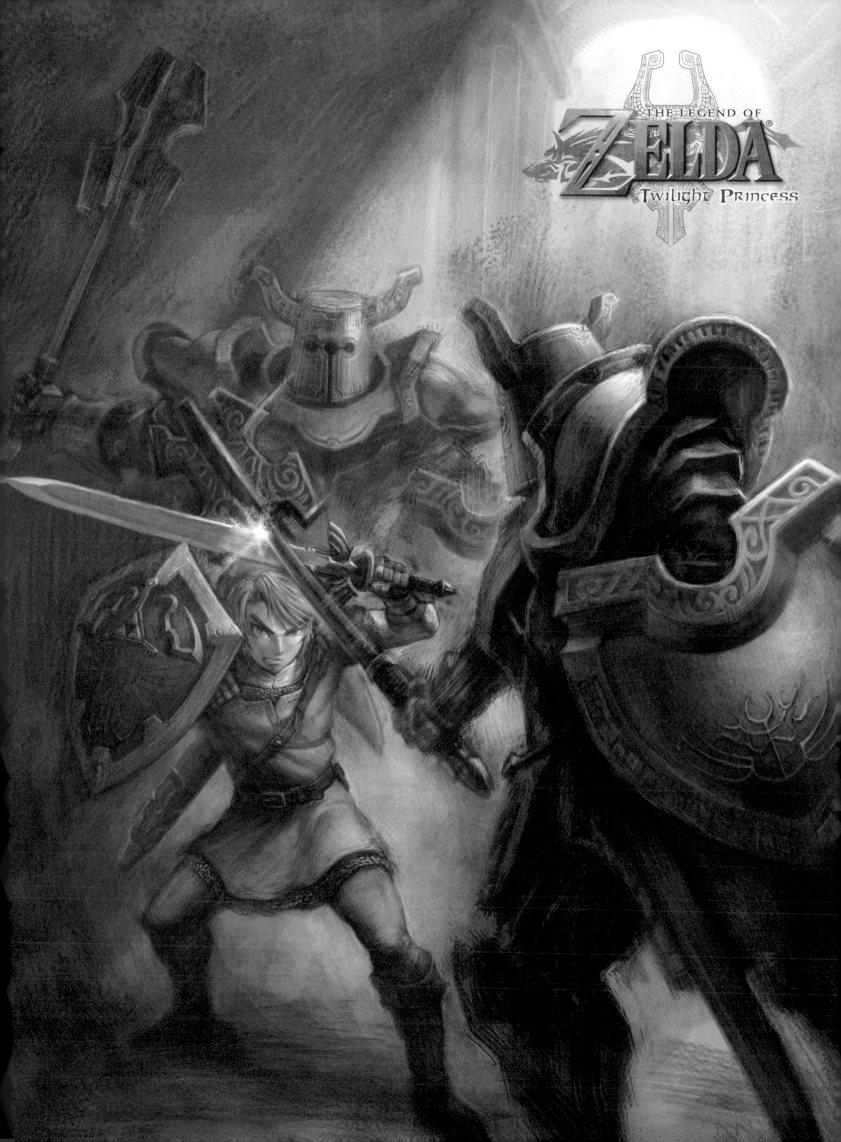

THE LEGEND OF ZELDA™:
Twilight Princess
HIDDEN VILLAGE

Piano arrangement by SHINOBU AMAYAKE
Music supervision by NINTENDO

Composed by TORU MINEGISHI

(Original Key : Bm)
(Original Tempo : ♩=138)

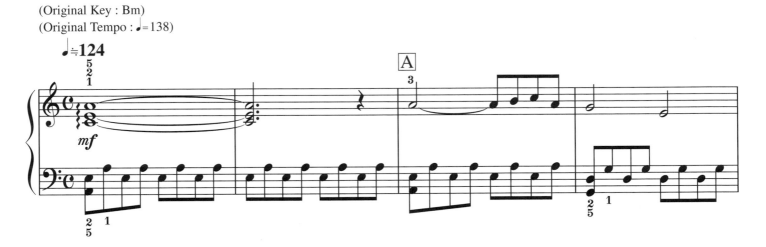

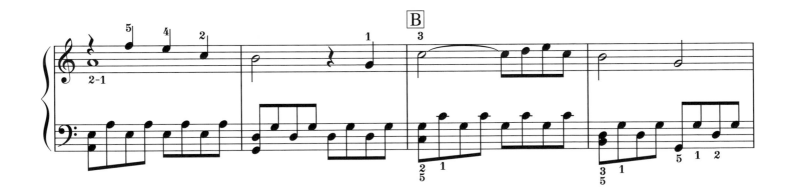

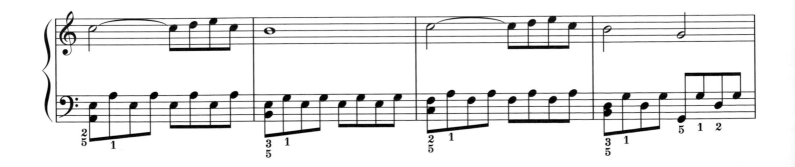

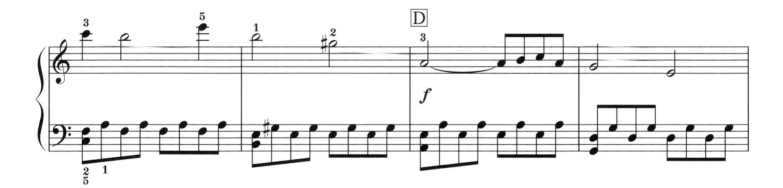

F.O.

THE LEGEND OF ZELDA™:
Twilight Princess
MIDNA'S LAMENT

Piano arrangement by SHINOBU AMAYAKE
Music supervision by NINTENDO

Composed by TORU MINEGISHI

(Original Key : Dm)
(Original Tempo : ♩=132)

♩≒116

(D.C.time 𝄐)

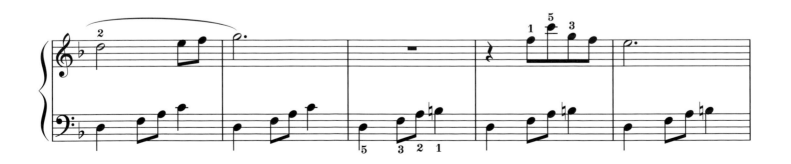

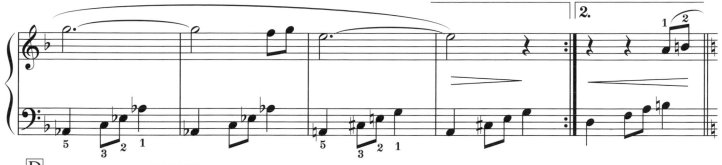

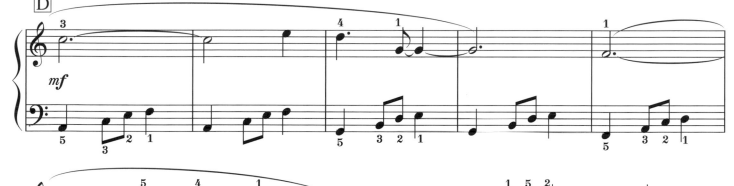

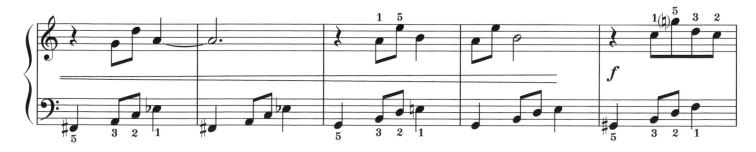

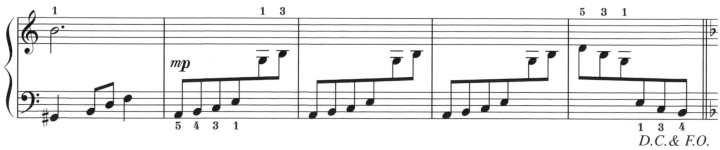

D.C.& F.O.

THE LEGEND OF ZELDA™:
Phantom Hourglass
CIELA'S PARTING WORDS

Piano arrangement by SHINOBU AMAYAKE
Music supervision by NINTENDO

Composed by KOJI KONDO and TORU MINEGISHI

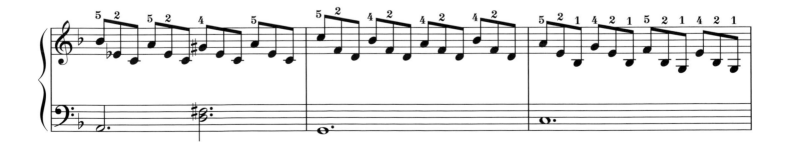

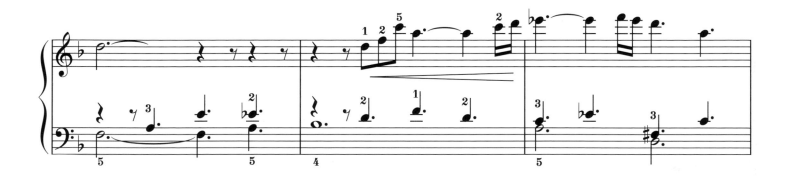

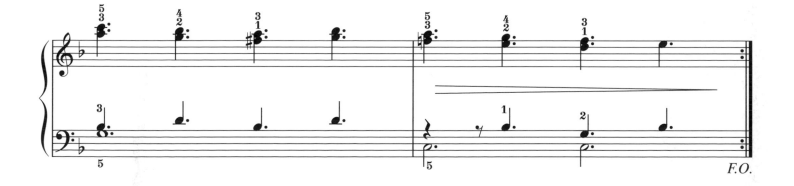

F.O.

THE LEGEND OF ZELDA™:
Spirit Tracks
TITLE THEME

Piano arrangement by SHINOBU AMAYAKE
Music supervision by NINTENDO

Composed by TORU MINEGISHI

(Original Key : A)
(Original Tempo : ♩=126)

♩≒108

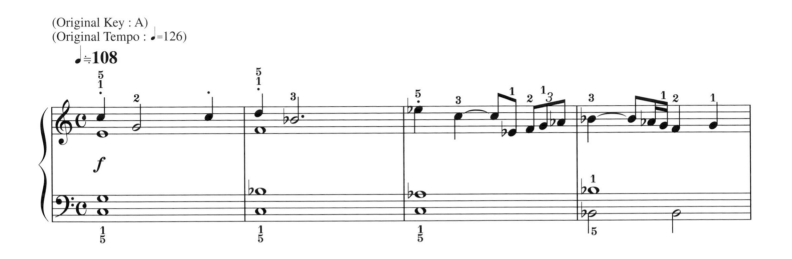

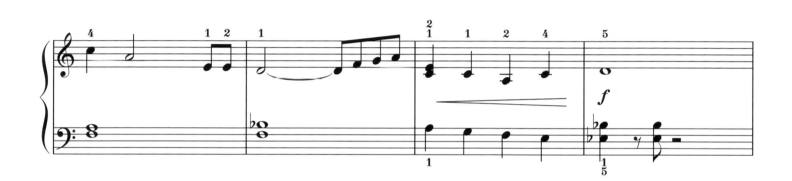

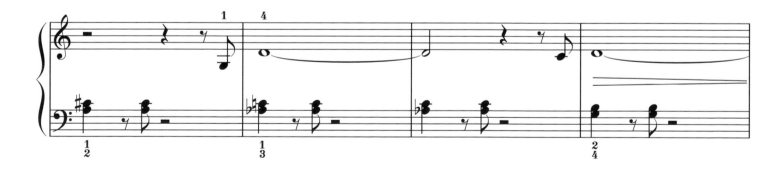

F.O.

THE LEGEND OF ZELDA™:
Spirit Tracks
FIELD THEME

Piano arrangement by SHINOBU AMAYAKE
Music supervision by NINTENDO

Composed by MANAKA TOMINAGA

(Original Key : C♯m)
(Original Tempo : ♩=96)

♩≒**70**

A

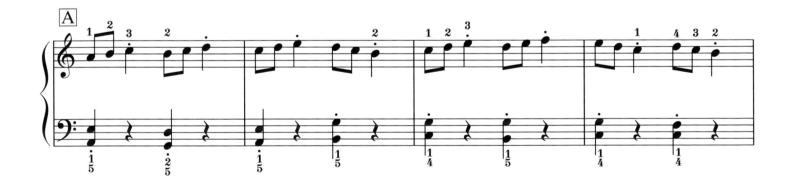

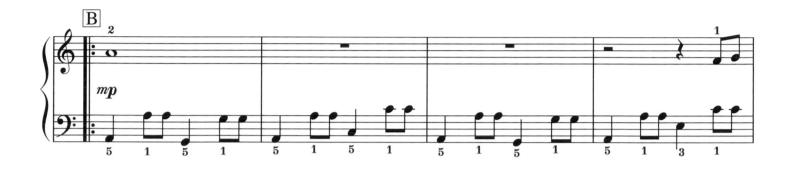

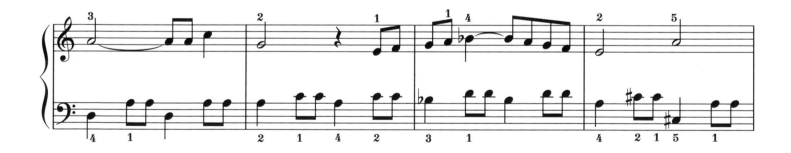

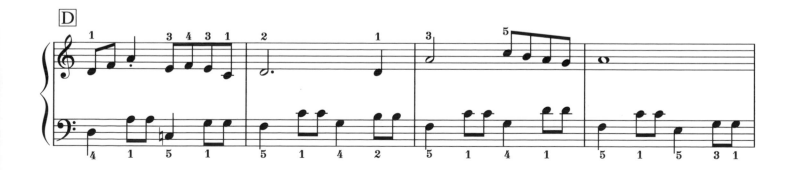

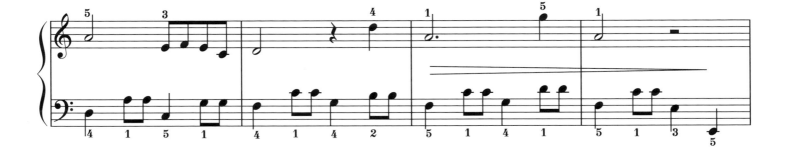

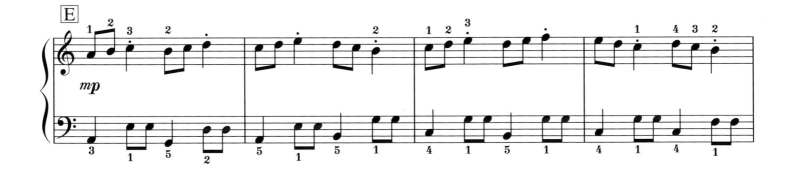

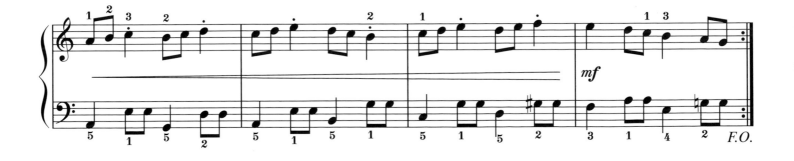

THE LEGEND OF ZELDA™:
Spirit Tracks
TRAIN TRAVEL (MAIN THEME)

Piano arrangement by SHINOBU AMAYAKE
Music supervision by NINTENDO

Composed by TORU MINEGISHI

(Original Key : Em)
(Original Tempo : ♩=138)

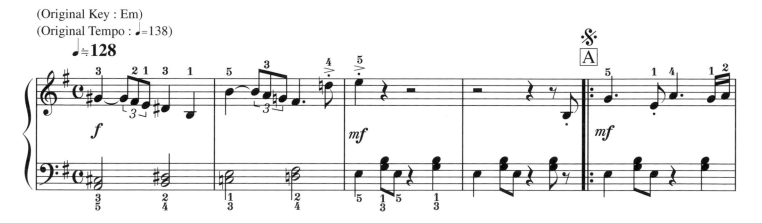

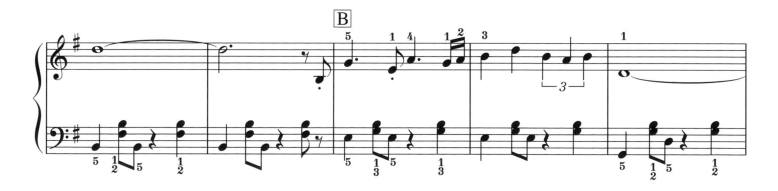

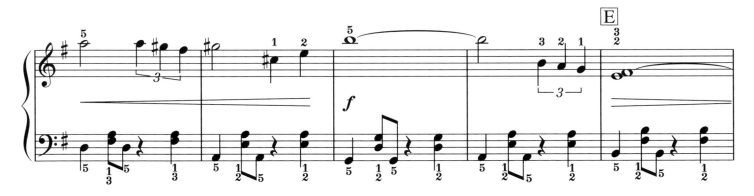

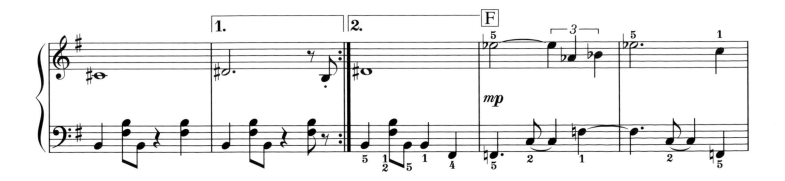

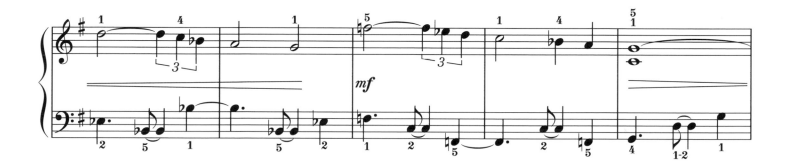

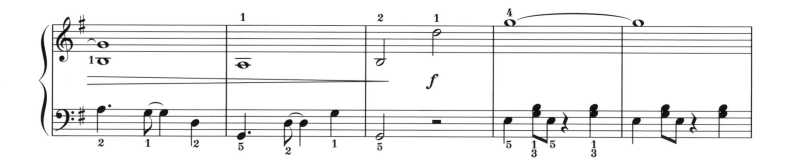

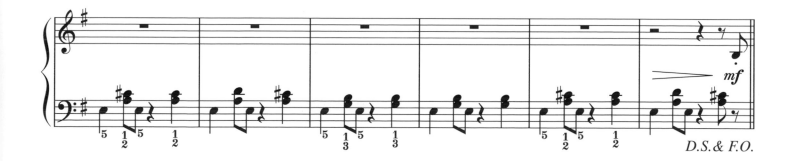

D.S.& F.O.

THE LEGEND OF ZELDA™:
TRI-FORCE FANFARE

Composed by TORU MINEGISHI
Piano arrangement by SHINOBU AMAYAKE
Music supervision by NINTENDO

(Original Key : G)
(Original Tempo : ♩=150)

THE LEGEND OF ZELDA™:
CORRECT SOLUTION

(Original Key : C)
(Original Tempo : ♩≒200)

Composed by TORU MINEGISHI
Piano arrangement by SHINOBU AMAYAKE
Music supervision by NINTENDO

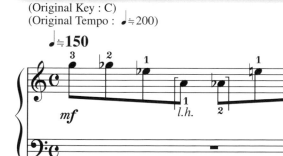

THE LEGEND OF ZELDA™:
WHISTLE OF WARP

Composed by TORU MINEGISHI
Piano arrangement by SHINOBU AMAYAKE
Music supervision by NINTENDO

(Original Key : C)
(Original Tempo : ♩≒100)

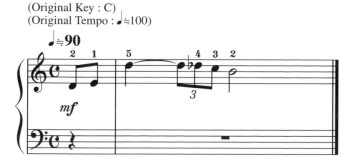